SUNDAY	MONDAY	TUESDAY	WEDNESDAY	THURSDAY	FRIDAY	SATURDAY
FOR AULD LANG SYNE, MOTHERFUCKERS.		31	1 NEW YEAR, SAME SHIT. New Year's Day	2 STILL FUCKING HUNGOVER. Day after New Year's Day (NZ, SCT)	3	4
5	6	7	8	9	10	11
12	13 STILL FUCKING WRITING 2024 ON EVERYTHING.	14	15	16	17	18
19	20 Martin Luther King Jr. Day	21	22	23	24	25
26 Australia Day (AUS)	27	28	29 Lunar New Year	30 ALREADY FAILED THOSE DAMN RESOLUTIONS.	31	1

OTHER SHIT TO REMEMBER:

❏ Try some crazy new shit.

❏ Make this year your bitch!

❏ Pay your bills and shit.

❏ Take down your fucking holiday lights already.

❏ Stop the shitstorm and make some resolutions.

CTRL
ALT
DELETE
THE BULLSHIT

SUNDAY	MONDAY	TUESDAY	WEDNESDAY	THURSDAY	FRIDAY	SATURDAY
LOVE IS EVERYWHERE. CUT THAT SHIT OUT.		28	29	30	31	1
2 ==RODENTS DON'T KNOW THE FUCKING WEATHER.== Groundhog Day	3	4	5	6 Waitangi Day (NZ)	7	8
9	10	11	12 Abraham Lincoln's Birthday	13	14 ==BITCH, SWIPE LEFT. YOU DESERVE BETTER.== Valentine's Day	15 ==GIVE ME ALL THE FUCKING CHOCOLATE.==
16	17 Presidents' Day	18	19	20	21	22
23	24	25	26	27	28 Ramadan begins	1

==**OTHER SHIT TO REMEMBER:**==

- ❏ Pay your bills and shit.
- ❏ Clean the shit out of your house.
- ❏ Chocolate is not dinner. Buy some damn groceries.
- ❏ Stop checking WebMD and go to the fucking doctor.
- ❏ Try some self-fucking-care for once.

WHAT'S ALL THIS

DUMBFUCKERY?

MARCH

SUNDAY	MONDAY	TUESDAY	WEDNESDAY	THURSDAY	FRIDAY	SATURDAY
AND SUDDENLY, EVERYONE'S FUCKING IRISH.		25	26	27	28	1
2	3	4	5 Ash Wednesday (Lent begins)	6	7	8 **FUCK THE PATRIARCHY.** International Women's Day
9 Daylight Saving Time begins (USA, CAN)	10 Public Holiday (AUS: ACT, SA, TAS, VIC)	11	12	13 Purim begins	14	15
16	17 **BEER SHOULD NOT BE FUCKING GREEN.** St. Patrick's Day	18	19	20 **SCREW YOU, ALLERGIES!** Spring begins (Northern Hemisphere)	21	22
23	24	25	26	27	28	29
30 Eid al-Fitr begins Mothering Sunday (UK)	31					

OTHER SHIT TO REMEMBER:

❑ You deserve a fucking vacation. Go plan one.

❑ Pay your bills and shit.

❑ Do your fucking laundry.

❑ Change your fucking clocks.

❑ Go see the damn dentist already.

GIVE 'EM HELL

SUNDAY	MONDAY	TUESDAY	WEDNESDAY	THURSDAY	FRIDAY	SATURDAY
DON'T RAIN ON MY FUCKING PARADE.		**1** CAN'T TRUST A DAMN SOUL. April Fools' Day	**2**	**3**	**4**	**5**
6	**7**	**8**	**9**	**10**	**11**	**12** Passover begins
13 Palm Sunday	**14**	**15** FINE, TAKE MY FUCKING MONEY. Tax Day	**16**	**17**	**18** Good Friday	**19**
20 Easter	**21** Easter Monday (AUS, CAN, NZ, UK except SCT)	**22** RECYCLE YOUR SHIT. Earth Day	**23**	**24**	**25** Anzac Day (AUS, NZ)	**26**
27	**28** Workers' Memorial Day (UK)	**29**	**30** SHIT. IT'S GONNA BE MAYYY.	1	2	3

OTHER SHIT TO REMEMBER:

❏ Pay your bills and shit.

❏ Your house is a clusterfuck. Clean it.

❏ Did you submit your damn taxes?

❏ Go fucking plant something.

❏ Bring your umbrella fucking everywhere.

EASY FUCKING DOES IT

SUNDAY	MONDAY	TUESDAY	WEDNESDAY	THURSDAY	FRIDAY	SATURDAY
MAY YOU ALWAYS GIVE ZERO FUCKS.	29	30	1	2	3
4 R2-D2 IS COOL AS HELL.	5 Cinco de Mayo	6	7	8	9	10
11 NOTE: MOMS ARE THE SHIT. Mother's Day (USA, AUS, CAN, NZ)	12	13	14	15	16	17 Armed Forces Day
18	19 Victoria Day (CAN)	20	21	22	23 HELL YEAH, THREE-DAY WEEKEND!	24
25	26 Memorial Day (USA) Spring Bank Holiday (UK)	27	28	29	30	31

OTHER SHIT TO REMEMBER:

❏ Is your shit broken? Fucking fix it.

❏ Pay your bills and shit.

❏ Call your fucking mother and let her know you appreciate her.

❏ Stop being a hot mess and get a haircut.

❏ To hell with work. You deserve a damn day off.

TAKE IT ONE

WTF

AT A TIME

SUNDAY	MONDAY	TUESDAY	WEDNESDAY	THURSDAY	FRIDAY	SATURDAY
1 Shavuot begins	2 **HAVE A CUP OF FUCKOFFEE, MONDAY.**	3	4	5	6 Eid al-Adha begins	7
8	9	10	11	12	13 **WATCH YOUR FUCKING BACK.**	14 Flag Day
15 **NOTE: DADS ARE THE FUCKING BOMB.** Father's Day (USA, CAN, UK)	16	17	18	19 Juneteenth	20 Summer begins (Northern Hemisphere)	21
22	23	24	25	26	27	28
29	30	1	2	3	**CUE FUCKING WEDDING SEASON.**	

OTHER SHIT TO REMEMBER:

❏ GTFO and get some damn sunshine.

❏ Pay your bills and shit.

❏ Buy your dad a fucking card.

❏ Get off your ass and go see some friends.

❏ Congratulate yourself for making it halfway through the fucking year!

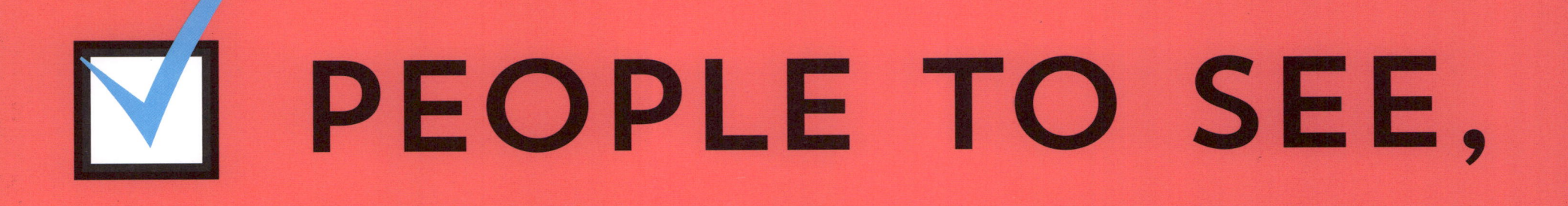

✓ PLACES TO GO,

✓ PEOPLE TO SEE,

✓ SHIT TO DO.

JULY

SUNDAY	MONDAY	TUESDAY	WEDNESDAY	THURSDAY	FRIDAY	SATURDAY
IT'S FUCKING LIT!		**1** Canada Day (CAN)	**2**	**3**	**4** LET FREEDOM FUCKING RING. Independence Day	**5**
6	**7**	**8**	**9**	**10** REALLY?! STILL FUCKING SHOOTING OFF FIREWORKS.	**11**	**12** Orangemen's Day— Battle of the Boyne (NIR)
13	**14**	**15**	**16**	**17**	**18**	**19**
20	**21** TOO HOT FOR THIS BULLSHIT.	**22**	**23**	**24**	**25**	**26**
27	**28**	**29**	**30**	**31**	1	2

OTHER SHIT TO REMEMBER:

❏ Fucking barbecue something.

❏ Pay your bills and shit.

❏ For fuck's sake, wear sunscreen.

❏ Buy all the damn fireworks and try not to scare every fucking dog in the neighborhood.

❏ Screw getting a beach body and have a fucking beer.

IT'S A FUCKING DUMPSTER FIRE.

SUNDAY	MONDAY	TUESDAY	WEDNESDAY	THURSDAY	FRIDAY	SATURDAY
SWEAT-FUCKING-CITY.		29	30	31	1	2
3 SNOOZE THAT SHIT! IT'S SUNDAY!	4 Summer Bank Holiday (SCT)	5	6	7	8	9
10	11	12	13	14	15	16
17	18	19 FUCKING COME AT ME, TUESDAY!	20	21	22	23
24 / 31	25 Summer Bank Holiday (UK except SCT)	26	27	28	29 HELL YEAH, THREE-DAY WEEKEND!	30

OTHER SHIT TO REMEMBER:

❏ Pay your bills and shit.

❏ Read a fucking book for once.

❏ Go have some fucking fun in the sun!

❏ Eat more damn protein.

❏ Handle your fucking business.

SLOW

YOUR

DAMN

ROLL

31	1	2	3	4	5	6
	Labor Day (USA, CAN)					
7	8	9	10	11	12	13
Father's Day (AUS, NZ)				Patriot Day		
14	15	16	17	18 **STILL. NOT. FUCKING. FRIDAY.**	19	20
21	22 **FUCKING PUMPKIN SPICE EVERYTHING.**	23	24	25	26	27
	Rosh Hashanah begins Autumn begins (Northern Hemisphere)					
28	29	30	1	2	**COZY MOTHERFUCKING SWEATER SEASON.**	

OTHER SHIT TO REMEMBER:

- ❏ Pay your bills and shit.
- ❏ Make this month your bitch!
- ❏ Summer is over. Put your fucking shorts away.
- ❏ You're not a fucking hermit. Go out for once.
- ❏ Start planning your badass Halloween costume now.

I DON'T FUCKING THINK SO.

OCTOBER

SUNDAY	MONDAY	TUESDAY	WEDNESDAY	THURSDAY	FRIDAY	SATURDAY
	SHIT'S SPOOKY.	30	1 Yom Kippur begins	2 R.I.P. THE LAST FUCK I GAVE.	3	4
5	6 Sukkot begins	7	8	9	10	11
12	13 HAPPY COLUMBUS-WAS-AN-ASSHOLE DAY! Columbus Day (USA) Indigenous Peoples' Day (USA) Thanksgiving Day (CAN)	14	15	16	17	18
19	20 Diwali begins	21	22	23	24	25 CUE THE FUCKING HALLOWEEN COSTUME SCRAMBLE.
26	27	28	29	30	31 SON OF A WITCH. Halloween	1

OTHER SHIT TO REMEMBER:

❑ It's not fucking Christmas yet. Put your festive shit away.

❑ Pay your bills and shit.

❑ Don't be an asshole. Buy some Halloween candy for the neighborhood kids.

❑ Candy is not dinner. Go buy some damn groceries.

❑ Trick or treat your badass self!

KEEP ON KEEPING ON, BITCHES

SUNDAY	MONDAY	TUESDAY	WEDNESDAY	THURSDAY	FRIDAY	SATURDAY
FUCKING GRATEFUL, THANKFUL, BLESSED!	28	29	30	31	1	
2 *FUCK YEAH, MORE SLEEP!* Daylight Saving Time ends (USA, CAN)	3	4 Election Day	5	6	7	8
9	10	11 Veterans Day (USA) Remembrance Day (CAN, UK)	12	13	14	15
16	17	18	19	20	21	22
23 30 St. Andrew's Day (SCT)	24	25	26	27 *FEAST YOUR FUCKING HEART OUT.* Thanksgiving Day	28 *AVOID THE ASSHOLE SHOPPERS. STAY THE FUCK HOME.*	29

OTHER SHIT TO REMEMBER:

❏ Pay your bills and shit.

❏ Make some festive fucking plans this year.

❏ Change your fucking clocks.

❏ Budget for the damn holidays.

❏ Start your IDGAF diet.

WHY THE FUCK NOT?

DECEMBER

SUNDAY	MONDAY	TUESDAY	WEDNESDAY	THURSDAY	FRIDAY	SATURDAY
30	1	2	3	4	5	6
7 Pearl Harbor Day	8	9 WRAP THOSE FUCKING PRESENTS!	10	11	12	13
14 DROP IT LIKE A FUCKING TOP. Hanukkah begins	15	16	17	18	19	20
21 WALKING IN A COLD-AS-SHIT WONDERLAND. Winter begins (Northern Hemisphere)	22	23	24 Christmas Eve	25 ENJOY YOUR FUCKING COAL, HEATHEN. Christmas Day	26 Kwanzaa begins Boxing Day (AUS, CAN, NZ, UK)	27
28	29	30	31 BETTER FUCKING LUCK NEXT YEAR. New Year's Eve	1	SEASON'S FUCKING GREETINGS!	

OTHER SHIT TO REMEMBER:

❏ Seriously, pay your damn bills!

❏ Trim the shit out of that tree.

❏ Bitch, bake some cookies.

❏ Stop being a lazy fuck and do your holiday shopping before the 24th.

❏ Fucking finally accomplish those New Year's resolutions.

ONWARD
AND
FUCKING
UPWARD!

2025